needle teeth

needle teeth

by thea taylor

Published January 11, 2026.

First paperback edition, printed by IngramSpark.

ISBN: 979-8-218-86723-2

Cover design, illustration, photography, and layout by Thea Taylor.

contents

An ode to the woes of abandonment.

bite

her

A young woman awakes stranded in the desert, soot smeared across her eyes and cheekbones. War paint to some; traces of despair to most. She finds herself in torn clothes, ribbons strewn about her swollen ankles as though she's a mummy risen from the dead. Opening her mouth to the pale blue sky, only a strained gasp escapes. Her voice has been scooped from tongue, scraped raw from her teeth. She rolls onto her knees and spits out blood.

A tooth falls out from the back of her mouth. She picks it up, dirt packed beneath her nails, and attempts to put it in again. It tumbles to the barren sand. She tries again and again until a wind picks up and carries it away, so easy like a feather. She scrambles to her feet, a foul taking its first steps.

She chases after the tooth, a silhouette on the horizon.

The woman leaves no tracks behind.

him

Across the way, there is a young man. A click of
bones and a hollow rib cage that peers out from the
shadow of his throat. His words rattle like a rock
down a well, falling further from him with every
aimless step. Poor attempts to rewind his life, but
the tape whirs and kicks, a blur of before—he can't
remember his voice.

The man has been walking in circles, confuses his
own footsteps for the trace of another survivor. He
sees a cactus in the distance and mistakes it for a pair
of arms, throws himself forward without thinking
twice. Needles cover him from ankles to ears, but he
doesn't peel himself away until his vision burns ice-
cold red.

He lay softly on his back, plucking the needles one
by one.

the duel

You are my huckleberry cowboy,
my brass knight with a swinging sword.
As the horizon burns from embers to ash, you
look at me funny—take me for the enemy.
Starting from the inside, then so delicately to
the out, you take barbed wire around my heart,
fill my bones with rod iron
until my blood goes cold.

I find no warmth
in arms anymore.

The sun fades from my face.
My skin is teacup porcelain, chipped
at the chin. Chapped lips to fangs,
quick into the nape of my neck.
I take a breath for another night
of your satisfaction—allow me
no grace. My only purpose is for
your growing pains.

I'm thread-barren, a rag doll with no shape.
Pull stuffing from your pillow,
mold my body to your liking.

No more than ten minutes. Take me out,
tear me apart, and start over with
the puppet you've been weaving.

You learned that pink is your favorite shade
of dress. Silk feels best on your skin, but lace
irritates the jagged edges of your doorframe.
Gets caught and torn.

Rabid dogs have a hunger that can be quelled, but
man knows no bounds. His stomach
is bottomless.

Here we are, trimmed and ribboned,
a bell rings, run on in—
we're ready.

Another feast for your
forgettable pleasing.

they say it's a curse

There was this particular color he loved:
the type of blue the sky churned before
a world-ending storm.

The kind where the wind knocks
against your windows, wood
starts to whine, and you wonder
if you are moments away from saying,
goodbye
to the home you were just so graciously
getting to know.

Maybe it wasn't blue—no,
it was this shade of gray.
So macabre, it reeked of death.
He had this fascination for those who
leave. You can't blame him—
your tenderness were bougainvillea thorns;
every love letter,
a cold sore.

It was easy for him
to get sick of you.

His words were ash-stained.

He meant it, or at least he wanted to.
Murmuring over candle flame,
an incantation asking for forgiveness.
He didn't actually intend for sympathy.
His memories are melted wax—
he adores this mold of you.
There and
gone.

A man of his making, dressed with
torn cloth and nosebleeds. An oil portrait
passed down. Ghost born
of limerence, he questions why
you want him to stay.

Why do you want him to stay?

roadkill connoisseur

When did my eyes get so big?
A deer in headlights, the world
never stopped spinning. On a carousel,
up and down, the height of your heartbreak like
a sail at high mass—too many cracks
to count, not enough reason to break.
Leaking at the seams, this life of mine—
it's not what I expected it to be.

My aim goes first to the hunter,
laced up in spotted furs, decorated with leaves and
supermarket flowers. Love loses color
against his skin: sullen,
teeth chattering, only hungry for more
plucked meat and hand-picked weeds.

I consider the bear,
who liked the corner of his cave
more than anything.
Leave tracks for me to follow,
I look up to an inky black cityline—
askew from the earth who knew
how to hold me right.

I flounder against asphalt, picking
through a stranger's hair in search of

roses and peonies. Floss poetry
from their gums until their lips
bleed.

These beasts of bones
fail to cherish the pink of the heart,
grow addicted to the stench of
a broken soul. So easy to take the pieces—
build from the ground up.

My eyes get bigger.
I'm on the run from
my next killer who promised
they were nothing like the others.

jack of all trades

I pulled an ace of spades,
thought about burying you.
Blame the devil on my shoulder,
it told me to play a trick on you.
I boxed up my trowels after
you used my stories as
paper weights—two century old linen
to clean a fish tank.

When I said, talking to you
is like writing a book,
you went silent—
flinched.

I should apologize for the way you
held on to my every word,
salmon on a hook, floundering
for more.

I shipped the shovels with no return,
drew skulls and crossbones
since loss doesn't scare you.

I won't wish you nightmares;
you're satiated off of pain.
Walk the tightrope of promises in which

you pushed me off. Like a dream
when the falling
does

       not

          stop.

I'll wake you up softly
with a spade to the head.
Maybe, you
would remember me
then.

velvet masquerade

In a room full of wolf masks, you
will find traces of wool—
the leather of sheep skin, broken nails
with mud caked beneath.
They tried to dig themselves from the grave.
Earth churned out evil:
out came
the people.

Cut down trees with three rings,
wear them on your finger, a reminder of
that kindred love of yours, fresh as
a daisy. New, shiny blooms—
spring's first bite. They've no idea
about those thorns; sickness molted
snake skins, chewed like a toothpick.

Look at how easily you become
exactly what they want.

The sheep learns to howl; the chicken
paints spots. Crack an egg,
full of nothing.
Bodies get thrown over,
skinned to marrow, keep their faces
as your newest memento.

lace playmates

Chocolate sponge with fig jam,
flowers of whipped cream, gold sugar pearls
that were promised to her.
Satin now sandpaper, buffed her fingernails into
fangs. Before dinner, the silver is polished,
crimson wiped clean. He forgets that she
has such sharp teeth.

Between the talons of the fork,
she imagines she has his neck,
starves for his love until delusions rise—
her hand being held.

The night is lonelier than him,
but none as empty as the
perfume bottle of her heart, squeezed
dry from paper-thin mornings. Lingering,
like laundry from childhood.

As she tosses and turns
the sixth time over, the moon
pours in—a swan's neck.
White light across her cheekbones,
a ghost with chattering teeth
provides her light, but she dreams for
the warmth of man.

God must've made a mistake
when He got to her spine.
Nobody fits around her—
they all feel like knives.

Dessert arrives, a pillow for her thighs,
diamonds for her ears to distract
from the eyes. She chips her tooth on
her favorite cake spoon.
He sweeps it under the rug—
passersby play along.

After all,
they just asked her to smile and
be nice.

wild is the prey

I dreamt I was a bird.
Pain was a feeling yet to be conceived.
Warm summer winds from a puckering June
climb beneath my feathers,
kiss my cheeks.

I follow blimps of dandelion seeds,
count every child's wish and stranger's
secret prayer. I've found that people
don't like to tell you what they need.
Love is this strange sort of
guessing game.

In my dream, I have two full wings.
I maneuver daggers of concrete and steel
until I am breathing in the sap of pine trees—
holidays where I watch stars fall to the dinner
table, see my smile reflected back in
emerald green bulbs.

I dreamt that I was free.
Pain was a myth.
A grandmother's warning, campfire
fables, broken street signs you
pass by and don't think twice.
I had only known life

as it was.

I dreamt I knew love.
The one made of angelic white innocence,
the rush of a late-night sugar rush.
When the tooth fairy never comes and you
get to keep your cavities as souvenirs—
a little girl's greatest fantasy.

Freedom means something different to you.
No bounds between the streetlights, yellow tape
waving in surrender, knotted around maple branches.
Tie feathers to chainlink, wear fur against
the scruff of your cheeks.

Not a thought crossed your mind as you
glared into the crosshairs.
A passing glance of an amber hide,
those big, bright white moon eyes,
once your savior, now a reason to
pull the trigger.

I'll know pain for a lifetime
all so you could collect
another piece of game.

hunger on the farm

The coyotes gather to howl into the night,
following a rabbit in disguise. Down
a blood-stained road to a cavern
once upon a time,
they called home.

Birthed from tender mothers,
the men gather their knives and bibles,
taken from the kitchen and their father's
nightstand. Leave behind the amber bottles,
shake the pills like an instrument;
men dance in the face of demise.

String up their innocence on the clothing line,
creased from tight fists, bodies dissected, and
torn away; a serial killer's wet dream.
The cattle herd together, praying for Noah's ark
to come around the bend. Part the sea,
whispered in a verse,
split with bullets.

Violence works quick. The farmhands
have little patience for
slaughter.

Blood runs thick with venom;
man is not quelled.

lady of the hour

He asked her to take a bite;
she smiled a mouthful of pomegranate seeds,
pulled rinds from the beds of her fingernails.
She'd wake a bear from hibernation
if it meant being in love.

It was cruel to take a girl
away from her window—
no mountain to trace,
no sun to follow. Wear shadows as
shawls, keep broken planets
around silver—the only
memento.

The night became her stockings,
easy to slip into—simple for him
to poke holes into. He'd paper mache the world to
her liking. She'd stitch poems
from broken promises, give the pain
a grand purpose. His deceit,
her royal crown.

If she was going to break,
she'd fracture the arctic, craft sculptures
of their love; they'd melt with
each passing day, the sun

tiptoeing close. Yet she will insist
his warmth
is all she knows.

Frostbite kisses her lips, caresses her legs.
She has to cut off her toes. Walking backwards is
easy, but moving forward means taking a fall.
She convinces herself she's better off this way:
Bitter oranges leave cavities.

Severed limbs
retain memories.

on the belt

My mother's kindness must've skipped
a generation—her patience
is lost on me.

I find my father's anger
rushing through my veins, boiling as blush
behind sun-kissed cheeks—alarm clocks behind
cat eyes. One wrong move, and
my adoration curdles.

Switchblade hatred:
your lies, the target;
our love, the bullseye.

When you yell,
a wounded child mirrors back, from your green
to my brown, the ground folding over,
like dirty laundry.

You lift the finger to the window,
spit venom on innocent faces,
I mimic your chant; you do it again.
We have this dance, breaking our knuckles
against glass. Ignore the familiar face
staring directly back.

Absence comes in a quick jab to
my rib cage, where your hand used to drift
in the unbuttoning of the night.
I glare at the empty space,
hate your guts—a knife without its napkin.

In the quiet, I hear myself rattling with fear,
watching my hands molt with blisters,
scrapes from curbs and concrete bowls,
knowing I am so close to becoming
the very one who took sawblades
to my soft edges.

I'm counting down the days until
the apocalypse, where we become
one and the same.

this is a robbery

Hands up!
Gold stars where I can see them!

I'll take your hopes and dreams just when
you thought you could see them.
Leaves turn to thorns. Cut yourself on asters and
marigolds—wear bee stings
as mother pearls. Learn
how to weave pain from Saturn's rings,
same as the scarlet letters
adorning your ribcage.

The garden you grew up in
feels like a fever dream.
Spend enough time in the desert heat,
you'll remember chocolate-dipped ice cream cones,
freckled west-coast summers,
sticky fingers, and sand
stuck between your toes. When youth
followed in footprints and laughter
echoed.

Death was merely a silhouette
at the edge of your bed.

Don't listen to what they tell you
while their eyes are flashlight red—
the monsters will find you beyond the night:
in the freezer section of the local grocer,
when a stranger offered you poison
disguised in a candy wrapper;
the cousin who broke the news
about the man on the moon.
Your childhood best friend
that looked you in the eyes and said,
God doesn't exist.

There's ink splatters on the day
they gave you the gun.
Hard to tell if it's a butterfly
or a bullseye. The shape is rage and you
have always loved the sharp edges of
hate.

It took moments for you to learn
how to point,
shoot, and
run.

Crush every piece of gold
into silver dust.

tiger stripes

She is cold and resentful, but prances the field like
brushstrokes—assuring the audience
she is forgiving. Keeps her love
locked in a cage. Swallows the key
just to watch her showmen beg.

Some say,
she has cannibalistic
tendencies.

They tried to take a nail file to her canines,
told her not to bite. The cuts on her ankles
speak volumes of another life.
Tied down, locked in chains,
given no girth for curiosity. Such a wild thing—
she deserves no
free reign.

Sometimes, in the underbelly of the night,
as the horizon seeps periwinkle and pine sap,
you'll hear a soft weeping from
the furthest corner of the cage.

Feral,
deranged,
for asking them to be
kind. She had to change her dialect,
and now, bares her teeth,
forces a growl from the base of her spine.
Rattling down until pain
makes pockets full of change.
Her knees buckle
with every leap of faith.

When she finds the will to put up
another fight, they sneak up
from behind.
Not strong enough,
she falters—
plays dead.

When they go,
she cries herself to sleep.
Prays for the day
she can be saved.

track & field

I left trails of tar along the highway, hoping you
would recognize my lip print,
come find and me.

I kissed the ground you walked on, mistook you
for some kind of god. Carried four leaf clovers and
dandelion seeds in my pillowcase, wishing you
would become the man of my dreams.

A mirage of angelic eyes, butterfly lashes;
I'm the only one to blame for your fleeting
seasons. Your roots once shared with others,
years on end, curdle at my touch
after a few months.

Bones of the sun, you burn
when the world grows cold.
Become molten,
rotten to the core.

murder in the sky

Nobody tells you that when Cupid shoots his arrow,
you get pinned to the peak of the sky.
Have no choice at all
but to eventually
take a

great

big

fall.

Sing me songs from the pond,
a warlock beckoning souls
gone astray. Trace my back so you
may dig a perfect hole
for my grave. Buttoned up in white lilies and
silk I can't afford,
you took me
for all my worth.

The casket does not catch me kindly.
Angel wings falter under the weight of
disdain—a carnivorous, ruptured sort of
broken heart. Thousand-year-old oak
caves under my splintered edges.

Few realize the cold of summer nights;
the sky above is a cruel shade of
rose.

When Cupid strapped me to the clouds,
I froze over. Became the rain so you
could live to see another day.

in lieu of absence

You took the ribbon from my neck and
tied it to our fingers, pinky to ring. Blame
your broken promises on my poor posture.
When you spun me around like a ballerina,
I found myself dizzy. Even the weight of you
could not tether me. I fell,
tripped onto my palms, tore through every
thread. Watched you get up, point
your finger, and
leave.

Plastic lace and ceramic blush—
I never liked dolls, but you
wanted a house. Brick by brick, constructed on
cracked pavement. Grout the tile with
every late night phone call. From the ground
up, we reach four feet high and
one foot wide. Not nearly enough to feel
your arms around me. Destined to fall,
built to distract.
Not to last.

If I can dream for another night,
between our bricks and stone, I'd lay
with the bed bugs, wrap myself
in cobwebs to remember the silken dress of

one true
love.

Conceptual relief with no critique.
Tainted and torn, pulled from the striped
sheets until I'm naked, left out to
wander the cold. Bones snap
on the first step. Stuff me with cellophane
to collapse at the next touch.

I'll be vague in your memory,
a ghostly reflection, bath towels
hanging from your bedroom door;
leaves falling from a tree, twisting
through the wind. You'll mistake it
for a dance when really, it is
trying so desperately to
escape.

paper weights

I spent all of my money on
borrowed time and books
you'll never read. Cinching up
laugh lines and stirling rings
that twinkled as you held
your morning coffee. Waited
in a rocking chair until
my knees buckled and my wrists snapped like
birch trees.

Fickle papercuts you avoided.
Baby smooth skin that pulled
thorns from my hips. An envy now,
watching you walk away, unscathed.

Keep your lashes to count wishes, fold
up your dreams like paper stars,
hanging from your bedroom walls.
I write stories of your youth;
slipping through my prose, running
egg yolks.

The dawn I miss, weave dreams to—
pray for the full moon. Pry my eyes open,
fill my bed with ink. I'm scared
of the light.

**You're the night
I'll never find.**

january eighteenth, twenty-twenty-five

If I could take one thing back, it would be the hope
you stole from me. I worked so diligently and
stubbornly to believe again—you felt like my prize
and my proof, and now I fucking hate you. I hate
that you are just another shadow rather than a wistful
memory. You are an example of why I can't trust
anyone.

My God, you are everything I'd hate to be, and who
I have been. You said you couldn't afford to get hurt
again, which is how I excused myself from failure.
It's sad and pathetic. I hope you're never really fully
happy because I don't think you deserve it. I think
you are all plastic and play. I won't say you fooled
me because I took a chance to believe. I wish you the
worst.

You, and all those who tried to pull me by the lead. I
don't want to be your training lesson so you can go
on to the next—give them the forever they dreamed
of. I hope they leave you high and dry. I hope you
stare at the ceiling and count your woes; I hope I'm at
the top of the list.

I hope you know real pain, and I endure this all for a
state of heaven that will grace me carefully.

swallow

The sun is his savior. It is in the light of the day,
the man awakes, no choice but to face the blinding
fire. He looks down, finding himself in a puddle of
his own treachery. Hands pockmarked with dropped
promises, legs cut from running too fast. The man
wanted so desperately to be held, but his fear reigned
strong.

When he was a child, someone let go of him along
the way. His skull cracked open on the asphalt, love
and likeness pouring out like an egg yolk. A neighbor
put a lunch napkin to his head, unaware of where the
damage was. Despite pointing to his chest, where his
heart was spider-webbing—fracturing wide open—
the neighbor said, "No, it's just your head."

So when the woman begs him to stay, drags the skin
of her knees until vultures begin to circle, the man
grabs her shoulders.

He looks her in the eyes before holding her close,
whispering in her ear, "It's all in your head."

She shakes her head.

"It's just your head," he says again.

her

None will believe it, but the woman is fully grown.
She babbles like a baby and misses her mother all
in the same step. Her tooth blows to the wind, a
tumbleweed. Cries come back to her—whispers over
her shoulders. They almost feel like a kiss.

Sadness becomes her romance—she mistakes
dewdrops for tears. Water is her sanctuary, pain
her security. The girl puts on makeup just to watch
the mascara bleed. Blinded by her insecurities, she
trips over what is initially mistaken as a rock. Looks
down, finds a carcass, picked over from scavengers.

For a moment, her vision cracks, as though she may
faint—she questions the pain in her chest, wondering
if she'd actually like to hurt again. A bandana to the
heart where there is no red to catch, she lets the sun
fall down and drape her back in shadow.

The skeleton falls behind. He becomes a sketch of
the horizon, a familiar silhouette of the sunset. A
toothpick in her mouth, she bites down until splinters
carve into her lips. She tastes blood when she smiles.

Looks at him and says, "Goodbye for now, but not for
long."

the desert is cold

Your home was plastic and overgrown grass—
pruned to give the illusion of home.
Warm arms snake around my waist,
rainwater eyes that glimmer
when the sun hits just right.

We meandered and danced around
your still-life of a living room with
furniture worth two months of rent.
Roll out the cow hide before I see
the rot underneath.

Tuck me in only for you
to turn your back in the night.
Watch shadows parade down the hall,
laughing as tears bruise my eyes. My purse
sits empty on the chair you posed me in.
A temperamental rococo,
curves you kiss, grab—
later,
erased.

I try to hold onto your fingers as they brush by,
a whisper along my hips. You vanish silently,
waves pillaging at midnight.

I ask what's on your mind, sculpt
statues from the distance in your eyes.
You say,
nothing at all,
crack a joke,
avoid a date for the
the plane.

You pack my belongings quietly,
not a postcard in sight, as if you
could tape me up in a box,
another name on your
mailing list.

Three months gone.
Will you tell me
how much has the grass grown?

Do you ever
mow the lawn?

shining knight

I had to drop my chainmail to your firefly
flickers of light.
Delicate and beautifully feminine,
my fear had no bearings—giving myself to you
was not even a question.

When I heard the steel bell toll
as you picked up your sword,
I convinced myself
you were something otherworldly—
of course you wouldn't hurt me.

A silhouette of my smile;
a shadow of my reapings.
Cut down the crop, feed the decay.
Walk away from an open door, climb a tower
Rapunzel herself
would fight you for.

My hands are made of glass.
I keep a shield taut, bone to bone,
on the skin of my back.

the smell of myrrh & a church

Silver at my collarbone and gold at
my throat, generations from before
with their thumbs to my neck—my voice
falls flat, slithering beneath state lines, waiting
for the next earthquake.

Dreams fall to ash, fate
billows to dust. The sun shines
only to remind me
what I have lost.
Persecute me for my lack of patience.
I stopped believing
before the age of sixteen.

Magic always made the most sense to me.
Flowers shaped like trumpets, music playing from
the trees. Dirt forming patterns, leaves
bristling in symphony. I swear—
they are speaking to me.

A hymn promising there is hope to be
witnessed—peceived.

Silhouettes of elbows in
mahogany, bright blue eyes in columbines.
Hair that sticks out like dill, curls up like

passion flower vines.
I tie myself in roots to
fathom reality.

But even nature cannot fight
the gruesome hands of man.

Sharpened steel and poison
in the shape of candy. Spraying smoke
to quell the hum of bees. Now they forget
the taste of honey. The dictionary narrows
and bitters, love
goes sour and the winter
becomes the Sahara.

Part the red sea, this lack of compassion you have
is not lost on me. I'll wear your pearls,
perch myself like a housewife, brown sugar
pressed at the corners of my lips as I break
the window sill, waiting too long.
Praying to this god who acts
as a guillotine.

Mass begins at midnight.
Blessings and peace to those

who neglect the origins of
community.

Mind your tongue,
but may you never
forget to speak.

mornings from a masochist

She walked the neighborhood at approximately
three-thirty in the morning,
white wine still on her breath.
Leaving a trail of tears, she made it
two-thirds of a mile. Out of breath,
by the time she reached her front door
again. Betrayal was her stalker—
she was getting tired of running.

In fact,
she was considering
succumbing.

They say, death is peaceful;
life is quite the chase.

She soothed her killers after their attempts.
Cuts on her palms, she held their hands, kissed
freckles of guilt from their face.
Waving away the lies like fruit flies.

Bopping for ivory, apples to her throat—
her heart withers a little more
from the inside. She avoids the doctor,
knowing they will look inside and say,
there is nothing left.

herb garden

Dead butterfly wings like lettuce
leaves; I used to starve myself until I realized
you could feed me.

Starting from the stem, down to petal
and pollen. Lick honey from the corner of my lips,
kiss beets onto my cheeks. Ignite the hearth
perched on my collarbone.

This warmth,
a poet's greatest whimsy.

Tie up your love at the spine,
backbone of desire, following
the footnotes like ivy—
once mottled to my skin, now a mark
of beauty.

The devastation man
has laid over me.

I could never collect enough thyme
for you to stay with me. Merry meet
with mint on your breath,
whisper sweet nothings
until our final breath.

if i could keep you in a jar

I would,
like the cocoons I found
gardening with my mom.
I'd scoop you with my palms,
poke holes into the paper on top.
Give you room to breathe,
since it seems you're so eager to leave.

I drop in fresh jasmine and rose petals,
whisper love poems; you break your teeth
on the chainlink
in a futile attempt to escape.

I trace the skeleton of your wings;
the carcass of your molting,
missing the man you could've been.

We meet again after metamorphosis, but
I don't think you've changed.
You paint your spots in pastels—
when the rain comes, the red of your heart
finds a way to bleed through.

I scrub my skin from crimson to pink,
until strawberry seed freckles sprout
along my shoulders and knees.

Fingernails polished with dirt as I
pull myself from the weeds.

I'm alive, and I think
it's real this time.

I keep you in a jar:
My treasure trove,
my memento,
you are everything
I hate about me.

x-rays

I think my bones snapped in half the moment
our eyes met. I knew I'd never walk the same again.
The careless skip in my step cracks my knees;
I've found myself in a freefall of dance.

You take me by the wrists. Tell me,
I'll never let you down.
The trees bleed into the streets, the sky and ocean
a pastel blur—every color becomes you.
I found purpose in beauty
once more.

Even when you left,
my edges were cotton-ball soft.
I'd understand everything
for the sake of your love.
The fingerprints of my reality
holding a heart to my daydreams; the floor
fell out from underneath.

I thought you'd come around and
catch me.

You're there and gone, love
a revolving door. When nobody is looking,
after I've tainted your name,

I press my hand to the glass—
find warmth
kissing the scabs on my fingers.

I'll never tell you, but my body would bend
to your will. Bruises on my heels
would happily blister
for another day with you.

life on mars

I have splinters under each finger,
gathering pine from mountain tops,
maple from fenced in yards.
I drug out water from the west to fill
your ever abundant abyss. Thumbtacks and
silver screws built this bridge. Each step
an exhilarating rush of the inevitable snap—
a hurricane eight
couldn't devastate your pathway.

We venture across, eyes swathed in black silk;
every day is night, harrowing
as a pack of wolves. Sky becomes the ground.
I fear birds for their freedom,
cower under the weight of song,
knowing your love was founded
on the fear of
never being needed.

I'm a foreigner among my own. Don't know
the language, can't find the words—
what does it mean to call someone
your home?

gone, but never left

There's basil growing in my windowsill
that you'll never see. Always reaching towards the
sun like
you'd never believe.

Remember what it felt like
to have a dream? When your arms
felt big enough to wrap around the world?
Take the snowglobe of your life,
shake it up. Plant trees in your bedroom,
make linens from a shooting-star wish.

Before you knew stars were dead planets,
winter branches mimic your lungs
after your first panic attack. Close your eyes
to the fright, let go of another night,
not a prayer in sight.

A hymn to the dove,
what was that you said
about love?

breakfast in bed

I put a grocery bag in my passenger seat
so my car would think there's someone sitting
next to me.

Two eggs, sunny side up, browned butter
toast made from the loaf of sourdough
you decided to loathe. Butter churned
from the stay in the mountains that
never came. Getting sunburnt
poolside, leaving the wake of our reality
far behind.

Watch the river run
along the spine you traced, whispered
sweet nothings to—leave traces of
searing iron and burnt tea leaves.
The heat from your palms
follows me as I climb
the tallest juniper to have ever
breathed.

Let me turn up the radio,
listen to your voice morph into
birdsong.

I hear you, echoing

along the interstate. A ghoul
hanging down from the streetlights.
Flicker from behind my eyes,
lightning strikes that spark
flame. Burn our house
down to ash before we
had the chance.

the river never ends

A thorn in his side,
splinters in his ribcage.
Her heart twists up, a thousand-year-old
water lily with gnarled roots,
knuckles bruised, punching through walls,
searching, searching, and—
there he goes.
Just as she predicted.
A glutton for writing the future
into fruition.

Clear crystal under her pillows,
she holds her breath, awaiting the signs:
stands in the doorframe that
he felt too big for; holds his hands
that carried her dreams like seeds.
Carelessly, let them catch
on the next breeze, a whistling from
the mesquite—they get stuck
in the floorboards like
popcorn kernels between teeth.

She steps outside. It is summer
again. The sun turns her cherry
red; she peels a layer of him
away. Honey curls out from

neighborhood trees. She tastes
sunlight, feels golden, and wonders
if she could be great.

gut wrenching

Having a banana at night
reminds me of being a kid,
sick with the stomach flu. Dizzy commercials
at two in the morning, dark figures
peering through the hallway and
the arched window from the front door—
unwelcome guests granting the treasure
of guilt, begging to be let in.

I can't keep a thing down,
pull the blanket over my head,
count to a number I don't remember,
willing the pointy faces far away.

I open my eyes to the dim dining room,
reality baring down—jagged wood and
antique chairs with arms that
mimic legs. Each familiar face
becomes a stranger.

There's my childhood best friend
plucking bundles of twenties from
a plastic bucket with my name and flowers
written in magenta ink. The beginning of
a girl's dreams in her life-savings.
My mom told me,

I was never the same.
A bruised heel that becomes a torn
tendon, abused from too many
missteps. I walk funny now.
My hip pops every morning.
I've lost count of how many lives
it's been.

How did my laugh lines get so thin?

Hurt gets heavier, hope
hurts. When my stomach turns over,
I think about crawling back into my mother's arms,
chewing on tortilla chips
to the lullaby of an infomercial,
when fear was a misshapen face
and my teeth only chattered
from a fever.

How resilient, the child;
how frail, the woman.

ignorance, no bliss

When the plane picked you up,
carried you like a crane over
the great, roaring waters,
did you even think of me?

As the clouds glared through
the porthole-shaped windows,
kites strung with destiny,
balloons floating from rose-colored
love, I must have crossed your mind.
Wandered the arch of your neck, pinched
your earlobe until you feel
a bite of pain.

If I knocked on your chest,
would I hear the sea sing back? Or would
the chords be cut, twisted nylon tied
backwards, playing every melody
wrong?

I find the blue of you
in everything, from the guitar
I gave up on to the ocean
we walked along. I murmured
over newspaper clippings, burned
string between two tapers to

break the curse.

I sold the guitar, folded up another dream
next to the memory of you. Put the money
towards my move. Even my home
was haunted by you.

When you play blackbird for her
in the dead of night,
do you remember
what my love felt like?

a mannequin shell

She sleeps with a pillow in her arms;
nothing makes her think of him more
than an empty bed.

Missing pin-drops in the hollow,
ricocheting like a pin ball machine;
she keeps playing, losing laundry quarters,
just to keep him with her.

She's addicted to grief.
Mistakes the swelling of sadness for
a balloon—thinks there's something
worth celebrating. It's a gift
to have loved at all. She knows
the five inch nail of longing, hammered
deep in her marrow.

He rattles in her hips
when she rolls out of bed; makes her teeth
chatter when the fluorescents go up and the night
becomes plastic. Quilted fists at her feet,
not sure why he had to
leave.

She falls asleep by staring into
the darkest corner—everything shallow
shares his eyes and nose.

the sunset of the apocalypse

The folks are selling their livestock, scraping
wood for chicken feed, beaks for pierced tongues.
The people are desperate for
song.

Call for the mother, weep
for the forgotten father—
a silhouette of your hooked nose and
buck teeth. Chew on hay, choke
on a pile of leaves. Change came around,
burned their love at the stake.
Fire, dynamite
red. They say the moon
knows better than he.

He who draws the earth flat,
puts stones in your pocket next to
a crumbled love letter. Pats you
on the shoulder, a friendly threat
before a single push
into the deep end.

Your shadow is quick to sink;
ink rises to the top.

he has risen

Hung at the wake of noon, strung up in
a pin-stripe jumpsuit. Tied
at the throat with a diamond necklace.
From this place, you were hoping
he'd see you.

Thorns pressed between thumbs like beads,
a gumball machine ring she returned
after another year gone wrong.
Ripe figs once lovingly chewed, now a trap
for horseflies. Sting of a hornet's nest
freshly adorned.

A delectable appetite for a hollow heart—temptation
for the wandering child who never got to read.
Told to go to bed without a wish of
good dreams. Fell asleep to the sound
of night knocking against their window:
dirty nickels and crumbs from the
passenger seat. Folk tales
get stuck in the creases; folded
into shoelaces to be tripped over.
Trample imagination to dust.

Run blindly towards fire, mistaken for
a star.

Out of breath, floating
from the ecstasy of what could be.
Put a stake in the ground, watch as sunflowers
root from cracked clay. Green
cuts clean through rope—
feet on the ground, alive with
crow's feet joy; tarnished wings,
strong enough for flight.

Falling, in hopes
he will pick you up.

tear-shaped lullabies

I sip on wine like a pacifier,
keep a web of gemstones close:
tiger's eye, black quartz, and
tourmaline to ward off the memories.

Stuck to my skin—pins and needles—
waiting for the shoe to drop.
Crush me like a spider; treat me
like your worst nightmare. I collect
lockets of firsts and late nights that end
with a quiet drive home.

I love you,
is a jump scare.

Claws around the doorframe, the boogeyman
under your bed only goes away
when you call for your mommy.
Slip away, a hand under the pillowcase,
cold like the winter we planned for.
Aloe vera and tea tree soothe
the wounds, but we itch the bites.
Bleed out unknowingly
from across the bedroom.

I line up rocks on my windows,

create spirals out of salt, and look
at old photos. Count calendar,
wishing you'd find me—
even the ghost of you
refuses to haunt me.

body flower

You smelled like sunscreen
when I picked you up from the sidewalk.

Suburbia was easter-egg-dyed cotton,
strung up to the sky that already felt
gold with spring. A surprise of olive oil
since I used the last drop for our dinner.

The first and only
home-cooked meal.

I had these postcard visions of us.
Nineteen fifties sort of perfection:
summers floating on the turquoise of
california lakes, the desert
leaving mosquito bites on my
knuckles and thighs that
you'd kiss away.

I never felt better. With you,
so easily, so simply—
I had been found. Your tortured,
lovely masterpiece
of a poet. Writing sonnets
after three hour phone calls, sending
pages, leatherbound.

What a tragedy when you
added my name to the page—
an escapade of history, traced
in the silhouettes of maids.
Mold my eyes over shoulder blades,
staring you down. Pain
hanging onto your elbow like
a barn owl. Wisdom arrives
after digging into your wounds.

The heat of your home left me feverish—
spinning in fleshy circles like
onion rings. Puddles of tears.
Slip and fall, crack my head, let you
in—flesh of my flesh—
make me into a shell,
hold it up to your skull.

My death gives you the courage
to swim again.

I waited for you
at the shore's edge. Now I am writing this
instead. Fulfilling the prophecy of fine china,
displayed bone
destined to crack.

Can I tell you that when I hurt,
I think of you? Wondering
what it would be like
if you were here.

Maybe I'd be happier if
I still had you.

84

acknowledgements

When it came to the creation of *needle teeth*, it felt
like death of sorts, being picked apart by vultures.
These birds were born of shadows from loss and
fear, after a short-lived relationship and a loss of
friendships. Big changes of the self that nothing can
ever quite prepare us for. I was reminded time and
time again how ugly humans can be, trying to hold
a tight, unyielding fist around love. This collection
was sprung out of hurt from others and anger towards
myself, often gathered in my phone's notes or written
across pastry bags and napkins from work. There
were times of pure hopelessness.

They were scary times. I toggled sharing many of
these poems. Some never made it to these pages.
They belong only to me.

I found strength in deciding to reassemble this
collection, despite the wounds within the pages,
whether of my own or observed. There were many
late nights balanced on glasses of wine, songs left on
repeat until I fell asleep. In some dark moments, my
shining light was laying out each page like I was Jo
March, bending over with a red pen and a hopeful
heart. That maybe, despite everything, there was
something worth saying.

The pain could take on a greater purpose. I could be honest with myself and reality without completely nose-diving down a dark road.

All this to say, I'm not entirely sure who to thank. I couldn't have done this without the support of my mother and sister, who have always believed in my writing. Even in moments when I have not felt good enough, they give me the reassurance to continue forward, reminding me why I love the pen and page so dearly. Thanks to their support, paired with the inspiration of great music, any story feels possible to pursue.

Thank you to the California desert for helping me realize how lost I was. Being out under the whispering northern lights helped me remember there is magic to be seen. It isn't such a bad thing, to not entirely know where you are going.

meet the author

Photo by Casey Eiland

Since the age of sixteen, Thea has been crafting novels of surrealism and greatly misunderstood characters. Throughout her time at El Camino College, she had several creative journals and poems published. Expanding to poetry and essays, Thea went on to self-publish, The Los Angeles Gardening Guide and Not for Show with Bottlecap Press. Both were released under her previous pen name, Thea Rosemary.

Thea is based out of her native city of Los Angeles, CA and lives with her rambunctious cat, Spirit. She is actively working on creating a community on her Substack titled, life's a picnic, where she features prose and thought-pieces. She hopes to bring perspective and inspiration through her stories, broadening compassion within humanity. When not writing, Thea can be found exploring new cafes, collecting old books she will never read, and baking treats for her loved ones.

www.ingramcontent.com/pod-product-compliance
Lightning Source LLC
Chambersburg PA
CBHW011239120626
46549CB00009B/3344